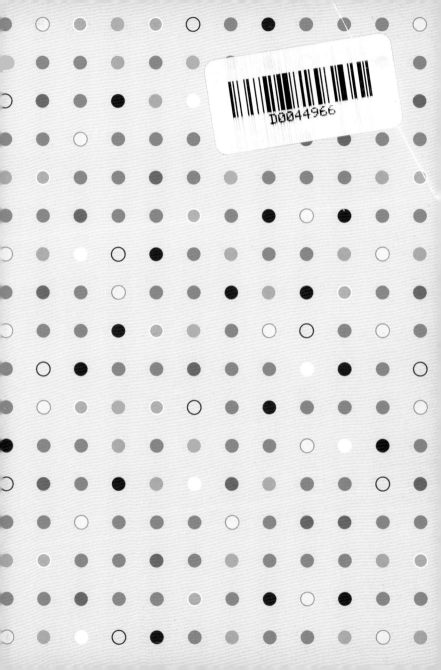

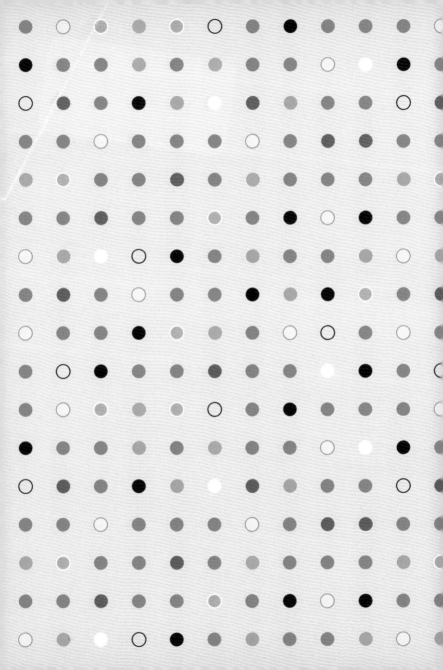

A gift for:

_____

From:

_____

Fancy Free!

Life Filled with Dazzling Hope

WOMEN of FAITH
BOOK SELECTION

COUNTRYMAN

Published by J. Countryman, a division of Thomas Nelson, Inc,
Nashville, Tennessee 37214.

Project manager—Terri Gibbs

Designed by Olika Design Studio, Cincinnati, Ohio, 45210
www.studiolika.com

ISBN-10: 1-4041-0407-0
ISBN-13: 978-1-40410-407-5

www.thomasnelson.com
www.jcountryman.com
www.womenoffaith.com

Printed and bound in Belgium

Contents

Free to Be Me!

Freedom—Loving Friends

Thankfully Free!

Acknowledgments

When I set God
at the center of my life,
I realize vast freedoms
and surprising spontaneities.

—Eugene Peterson

FORGIVEN AND FREE

Belonging to God is liberating.
It sets us free and
satisfies our longings.

—Mary Graham

Freed by God's Love

*A*ds and marketing people will tell you that you are your stuff. You are what you drive. You are what you wear. You are the number on the bottom of your bank statement.

Your conscience will tell you that you are your past. You are the sum of your choices, many of them wrong ones with difficult consequences.

Your mind will tell you that you are your fears. You are the sum of your worries about the future and if you just think about it enough, surely you can figure it out and short-circuit the impending disaster.

But Jesus said that real life is none of these things.

You are not your stuff.

You are not your past.

You are not your fears.

12

You are someone He loves unconditionally, someone He sacrificed His own life for, someone who matters very much to Him and to the people in your scope of influence. No matter what you have or don't have, no matter what you've done or not done, no matter what unknowns stretch out before you, you can know this: God loves you so much and He longs to make Himself at home in your life. Will you let Him?

When you experience His love and forgiveness, you will begin to understand what it means to be a person who has nothing to lose, nothing to prove, and nothing to hide.
That's real freedom.
That's real life.

—Anita Renfroe
The Purse-Driven Life

NOW YOU ARE FREE
FROM SIN. . . .
THIS GIVES YOU LIFE
FOREVER.

ROMANS 6:22 NCV

The Freedom of God's Forgiveness

When we misbehaved, my mother would say to us, "Say you're sorry." I never knew why that was important. I rarely felt sorry.

Now when I become aware of sin-actions or attitudes that aren't according to God's Word— I agree with Him that I'm in the wrong, acknowledge His forgiveness, and move on.

He deals with all sin the same way. He deals with all people who sin the same way.

He died for everybody's sin. All sin. We experience the freedom of His forgiveness when we stand in agreement with Him. It's like saying we're sorry. The Bible calls it confessing.

—Mary Graham
Women of Faith Devotional Bible

God Is for You!

Christ takes away your sin, and in doing so, He takes away your commonness. No longer need you say, "No one knows me." God knows you. He engraved your name on His hands and keeps your tears in a bottle (Isa. 49:16; Ps. 56:8). . . .

God knows you. And He is near you! How far is the shepherd from the sheep (John 10:14)? The branch from the vine (John 15:5)? That's how far God is from you. He is near. See how these four words look taped to your bathroom mirror: "God is for me" (Ps. 56:9).

—Max Lucado
Cure for the Common Life

GOD IS FOR ME!

Let Your Heart Be Free

When I was a little girl, my sister and I had been petting goats in our neighborhood park. One of the goats was hungry and became convinced that I was holding out on him. He stuck his head in my pocket and bit on something that smelled vaguely like food to him. He couldn't get his nose out, and he wouldn't let go. My sister told me to take off my coat, but I refused because it was my cool new green duffel coat. I ended up having to go home through the park with a goat attached to my coat.

When you won't let go of unforgiveness or bitterness, it will take you places you won't want to go. It will keep you tethered to an event that is long gone. Your heart will never be free until you let go.

—Sheila Walsh
The Heartache No One Sees

God wants you to fly.
He wants you to fly free of
yesterday's guilt. He wants you
to fly free of today's fears.
He wants you to fly free of
tomorrow's grave. Sin, fear, and
death. These are the mountains He
has moved. These are the prayers He
will answer. That is the fruit He will
grant. This is what He longs to do.

—Max Lucado

Free to Forgive

*W*hen we make a mistake, we aren't expected to grovel our way back into God's good graces. We're privileged to march up to His throne of grace *boldly*, not hanging back, not whimpering and whining, but *boldly* coming before Him. . . . Is our God a great God, or what?!

But here's the hard part, honey: God expects us to extend the same grace and forgiveness to those who offend us. That's right. We're supposed to forgive the ones who hurt us, insult us, and wrong us. . . .

Let me confess right here: sometimes I get mad at people, and I have a hard time getting over it. They did me wrong, girl! They hurt me, and I want to hurt them back. . . . But Jesus has told us to forgive those who sin against us. . . .

When Jesus told His disciples to forgive those who had wronged them, they replied, "Give us more faith" (Luke 176:5 MSG).

They asked for help, and so do I.

—**Thelma Wells**
Listen Up, Honey

GIVE US
MORE
FAITH.

God is big enough
to do the things
you have labeled impossible.

—Kathy Troccoli

Reach Out in Love

$\mathcal{E}$very night when I tuck my son into bed I ask him this question, "Which boy does Mommy love?"

He will put his hand on his cheek and reply, "This boy!"

May I suggest that every time you catch your reflection in a mirror you ask yourself this question? "Which girl does Jesus love?"

Put your hand on your cheek and say with absolute confidence, "This girl!"

One of the greatest struggles we will face on this earth is forgiving those who have wounded us. We can't do it on our own, but God's outrageous love teaches us how to forgive. It is God's gift to us to help us live in a world that is not fair. Let's turn our hearts now to those who have wounded us and ask God for the grace to extend forgiveness.

—Sheila Walsh
Outrageous Love

Free from Guilt

In 1966 the British Broadcasting Company ran a
spoof on one of their nightly TV news programs. It
was a five-minute documentary on the complexities
of spaghetti-growing in Italy. Without the slightest
hint of humor, the announcer told the audience that
throughout Italy millions of pasta farmers were
working harder than ever before to harvest their
pasta before it fell prey to the pests that ravaged
much of last season's crop. Footage showed farmers
in broad-brimmed hats working their way up neatly
trimmed aisles of spaghetti trees in the Italian
farmlands. . . . This report was made to the BBC
viewers with no reference to satire or levity.
Apparently millions of them did not question the
fact that spaghetti grows on trees.

As improbable as it might seem that people would
swallow that tall tale, some of us swallow equally
tall tales about ourselves. We believe that if we don't

look attractive, seem intelligent, smell good, and have matching clothes, we ought to stay in the house. . . . We also believe that if we make mistakes, the yard turns brown, . . . we wear green shoes with a navy suite, and we're fired from the job, we have no value . . . no worth. . . . We feel guilty: If the truth were known, it's our fault the rain won't let up; somehow everything that's wrong in life can be traced to something we're doing wrong. . . .

Although healthy guilt can be a positive motivator for change, unhealthy guilt, which hooks up with unhealthy shame, can huddle in our hearts and make us miserable and ineffective. These guilt patterns have the potential to sabotage productivity, stymie development, and silence our authentic voices. When that occurs, we've taken our eyes off of Him who longs to set us free from the bondage of guilt.

—Marilyn Meberg
The Zippered Heart

The call of outrageous
love is to abandon all
personal agendas
and to follow Christ
with glad hearts.

— Sheila Walsh

Free from Mistakes and Failures

When they were growing up, I taught my kids, "Don't make the same mistakes everyone else makes. Learn from their example. If you're gonna make a mistake, let it be something original. If you're gonna mess up, don't make the same mess twice. If you're gonna fail, fail at something new."

Yes, ma'am, that's the lesson I taught my kids: learn from your mistakes. And then I went right out and repeated the same mistakes myself. . . .

Thank God that He uses our mistakes to make us better. He uses "the stone that the builders rejected" (the unlikely, the misfit, the flawed, the failure) and makes it His "chief cornerstone" (the role model, the leader, the mentor). That's you and me, honey! In this life, we'll always be imperfect. But, through God's good grace and glory, He uses us anyway! He uses our mistakes, even when we make the same ones over and over.

—Thelma Wells
Listen Up, Honey

What an amazing exchange! We give God the filth of our lives, and He gives us liberty — the freedom to live and have our being in His love and forgiveness — while He makes His home in our hearts forever!

— Lana Bateman

A Holy Potpourri

I'm impressed with the rose because of its fruitful existence. It begins as a bud, which has a beauty all its own; gracefully unfolds into velvet overlays; and then, with its last breath, when crushed, it leaves a heady fragrance and drips precious oil.

As we consider the beauty and grace of the rose, we're not surprised to discover that Jesus is called the Rose of Sharon. He was born a bud of a babe in a manger; His beauty unfolded before others with each humble step He took; and in His last breaths on earth, with thorns pressed into His head, after being crushed by our sins, He shed precious drops of His blood and released a forever fragrance of love. . . .

That sacrifice, Christ's broken body, now calls us to receive the crushing blows of life as a way for His fragrance to be released through us — a holy potpourri. Take a shattered heart, mix with a crushed spirit, intermingle with Christ's oil of mercy, stir with His healing touch, and season with divine love.

—Patsy Clairmont
All Cracked Up

God's Great Surprise

*T*his is the great gift that Christ brought all the way from the very courts of heaven to the streets of Jerusalem, Capernaum, or Chicago:

I forgive everything — live differently.

The outrageous message was not, "I forgive you, so go and live any way you want." Neither was it, "Because of how you have lived there is no forgiveness." The glorious message, God's great surprise, was that everything about us is known and can be forgiven through Christ's sacrifice — and through the power of the Holy Spirit we can live differently.

— Sheila Walsh
Outrageous Love

LIVING FREE

Freedom means life
controlled by truth
and motivated by love.

—Warren W. Wiersbe

When we trust God
we are free to rely
entirely upon Him
to provide
what we need.

—Richard Foster

Free to Follow Christ

We are all travelers, whether we want to be or not. Life forces us to hit the road in search of doctors, banks, dry cleaners, groceries, and many other things. Les and I divide our time between Texas and Michigan, which means for me, a non-mapper, that I seldom know where I am, much less where the bank is in relationship to our home. So sweet Les, in an attempt to simplify my perpetual lostness, chose the bank directly across the street from our subdivision. No missing piece there — out the driveway, into the bank. Now, if only life were that simple!

Thank heavens for Jesus, who offers to walk with us wherever we are. He promises to guide our steps and light our path. Jesus is there for us if, like Zacchaeus, we are out on a limb. He's there for us if, like Eve, we've taken the wrong path. He's there for us if we are wandering aimlessly or high-stepping with certainty.

—Patsy Clairmont
All Cracked Up

Set Free

We lose our way. We want hope. We want forgiveness. We want restoration. We want freedom.

We must continually take trips to the cross. We must live a life of repentance. We must keep our hands open so that God can fill them. He will forgive. He will restore. He will set free.

—Kathy Troccoli
Hope for a Woman's Heart

God Holds Our Future

$\mathcal{B}$ruce Larson tells a story about a man who was taking a cruise on an ocean liner. Somehow one of his socks got away from him and blew over the railing, forever lost. Without a thought, the man flipped the other sock over the railing too. He knew when he was looking at a hopeless situation.

In contrast, many of us would take the remaining sock home and KEEP it, hoping a mate might miraculously turn up sometime. But all we would be doing is cluttering up our sock drawer. Instead, like the man on the ship, we need to let go of the painful situations that are out of our control and step out, unencumbered, knowing God holds our future in His hands.

—**Barbara Johnson**
Daily Splashes of Joy

I Choose to Believe

I've lived by myself for the past thirty years, and it's been an interesting adventure. More often than not, there's been nobody in the wings to come to my aid financially, nobody to pick up the slack or run errands, . . . nobody to lift me out of the doldrums. Humanly speaking, all responsibility ultimately has fallen on me. Some days I feel OK about this; other days I don't — I feel overwhelmed. . . . I can choose to let my overwhelming feelings guide my behavior (and sometimes I do), or I can choose to believe that God is with me and caring for me and teaching me lessons I couldn't learn any other way.

If I choose to live out of my emotions, no telling what might happen or where I might go to salve my depression, dissatisfaction, or discouragement. Feelings fluctuate with the day, the wind, my hormones, circumstances, and human relationships. But because God told me He doesn't change, I can choose to believe Him no matter how I feel.

— Luci Swindoll
I Married Adventure

A Worry-Free Life

Do not worry about anything,
but pray and ask God for everything you need.

Philippians 4:6 NCV

Some of us have postgraduate degrees from the University of Anxiety. We go to sleep worried that we won't wake up; we wake up worried that we didn't sleep. We worry that someone will discover that lettuce was fattening all along. The mother of one teenager bemoaned, "My daughter doesn't tell me anything. I'm a nervous wreck." Another mother replied, "My daughter tells me everything. I'm a nervous wreck." Wouldn't you love to stop worrying? Could you use a strong shelter from life's harsh elements?

God offers you just that: the possibility of a worry-free life. Not just *less* worry, but *no* worry.

—Max Lucado
Come Thirsty

To believe in a miracle
is only a way of saying
that God is free—
free to do a new thing.

—Eugene Peterson

We Choose to Laugh

When we're trapped in impossible predicaments we don't have a lot of choices. Our lives seem to be controlled by whatever blow hits us next, sending us lurching from headache to heartache to horror story. But we *can* choose how we respond emotionally. We *can* choose to hold on to the One who promises never to leave us, no matter how insane our schedules get.

And we can choose to laugh.

Now, I know very well that being a joyful woman can sometimes be a challenge. . . . What I'd really like to do when the plane is late or the luggage is lost or the elevators aren't working is get upset — start whining and moaning. Other times I want to be mad; I want to raise my voice, harden my heart, tighten up my face, and unload a sharp tongue-lashing to whatever unfortunate soul happens to cross my path at that moment. But, frankly, I've tried those choices and neither one is satisfying. Oh, sure, there's a momentary release of pressure as I vent my frustration and speak my mind. But just as quickly I regret my thoughtless words and harsh remarks.

And yet, I can't remember *ever* regretting a kind word I somehow managed to share in tense times. Or a smile I forced onto my lips when I really wanted to scowl. Or a giggle that bubbled up instead of a complaint.

—Barbara Johnson
Leaking Laffs Between Pampers and Depends

Laugh! It's like jogging on the inside.

—**Barbara Johnson**

Laugh-lines
from Barbara Johnson:

 A rule for women that has no exceptions:
If it has tires or testosterone, you're gonna
have trouble with it.

 Veni, vedi, visa
Translation: I came, I saw, I did a little shopping.

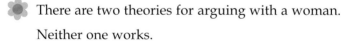 A good way to have the last word . . .
is to apologize.

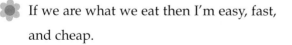 Wise husbands know that PMS is Mother Nature's
way of saying, "Get out of the house!"

 There are two theories for arguing with a woman.
Neither one works.

If we are what we eat then I'm easy, fast,
and cheap.

Experience is something you don't get until just
after you need it.

Free to Live a Simpler Life

"Less is more" has become a popular mantra in our society. I'm not convinced it has caught on in actuality, but it does have heads nodding in agreement. It's as if the bobbing of our noggins makes us appear savvy, but in truth many of us continue to live stuck in the muck of plenty. For instance, a second vehicle, as convenient as it is, requires insurance, maintenance, and pricey gas. It takes up valuable space in the garage and driveway, and it's always parked in the wrong spot when you need it. . . . Is it worth the hassle and frustration?

I'm starting to sense that many of our itches, twitches, lumps, and bumps may be brought on by our own choices to dive into society's pool of muchness. We sometimes need to be reminded what a worthy use of our time backyard gardening is, how rejuvenating a swing in the hammock can be, how relaxing a good read is, and how invigorating it is to stroll through our own neighborhood. . . .

I'm not so naïve as to believe that if we trimmed back on indulgences we wouldn't have tension. I just wonder if we're not adding unnecessary pressure to our already challenging stint here on earth with our pleasure-seeking, stuff-gathering tendencies.

—Patsy Clairmont
All Cracked Up

MY TIMES
ARE IN
YOUR
HAND.

Psalm 31:15

Free from the Tyranny of Time

*W*hen I look back through thirty years of journaling, on almost every page I've written something about not having enough time. And the truth is, I'll never have enough time because it's all up to God, and He views time differently than I do.

My time has to do with *duration*, a measurable period when something occurs. I don't have enough "duration" during the day. I lack the continuum for everything I want or need to do to actually get it done. It's that simple. But God's timing is in terms of *division*; He operates moment by moment or through seasons or a lifetime or a dispensation. His time is not measurable, because He's eternal and earthly time is temporal.

The reason this is important is because when I look at my life from a human viewpoint, I run out of time. But when I look at it from a spiritual viewpoint, I see that God is in charge of everything; I'm not! Therefore, He's in charge of my time.

— Luci Swindoll
Life! Celebrate It

Practicing Kingdom Customs

I live in a houseful of aliens — three males and just one reasonable, sensible female . . . me.

When I think about it, though, I realize being an alien isn't so bad. Being queen of the manor can be pretty nice sometimes.

In a general sense, being an alien simply means you have no permanent ties to the place you live. And shouldn't that describe us as believers? . . .

As sojourners, our customs are not those of this world; they're kingdom customs.

* When the world tells us to keep a big chip on our shoulders and make our violators pay dearly, our custom is forgiveness. (Matt. 6:14) . . .

* When the world tells us to "look out for number one," . . . our custom is sacrificial compassion. (Col. 3:12)

When the world tells us to get all we can, buy now and pay later, and go for the gusto, our custom is wide-open generosity. (Matt. 5:41—42)

When the world tells us to "just do it," our custom is self-discipline. (1 Pet 1:5—8)

When the world says you can "have it your way," our custom is altruism and humility. (Phil. 2:13) . . .

To practice this kind of countercultural living is to conform to the culture of heaven, the country of our real citizenship.

—Jennifer Rothschild
Lessons I Learned in the Light

Freedom from Fretting

$\mathcal{T}$his will probably come as a shock to most of you, but I am not a very patient person. I hate to wait! Of all the jobs and responsibilities and activities I have going on, the hardest things I do are wait for a doctor's appointment or wait for an overdue airplane or even wait for my nail polish to dry. Honey, I have places to go, things to do, and work to finish. . . .

If you're one who, like me, tends to get impatient when you're forced to wait and wait and wait, consider changing your *maditude* to *gratitude*. Instead of fretting about the time you're wasting and all the things you have to do, take advantage of the break you've been given.

Close your eyes and pray, "Thank you, Lord, for giving me this time to rest. I'm overwhelmed with all the things I have to do and the things I want to do, and I know I don't have time for all of them. Help me to shift my focus away from those long lists of have-to-dos and want-to-dos." . . .

If you're not a porch-swing person, ask Jesus to give you an image of your favorite relaxing place where you can mentally and physically take a break and step back from the hustle-bustle world.

—Thelma Wells
Listen Up, Honey

Every woman
has the ability
to choose
hilarity or insanity
on a daily basis.
Choose laughter.

—Anita Renfoe

I will greatly rejoice in the LORD,
my soul shall be joyful in my God.

Isaiah 61:10

Da Vinci painted one Mona Lisa.
Beethoven composed one Fifth Symphony.
And God made one version of you.

—Max Lucado

Free to Fulfill God's Purpose

God planned and packed you on purpose for His purpose. . . .

You are heaven's custom design. God "formed you in your mother's body" (Isa. 44:2 NCV). God determined your every detail. . . .

At a moment before moments existed, the sovereign Star Maker resolved, "I will make _____." Your name goes in the blank. Then He continued with, "And I will make him/her _____, _____ and _____ and _____ and _____." Fill those blanks with your characteristics. Insightful. Clever. Detail oriented. Restless. And since you are God's idea, you are a good idea. What God said about Jeremiah, He said about you: "Before I made you in your mother's womb, I chose you. Before you were born, I set you apart for a special work" (Jer. 1:5 NCV).

Set apart for a special work.

—Max Lucado
Cure for the Common Life

Beautiful in Time

$\mathcal{B}$ecoming the person God longs for us to be doesn't happen easily or quickly. No one waves a magic wand over your head and — voilà! — the Proverbs 31 woman emerges. It's a process of walking each day with Him, asking Him to penetrate your soul, giving Him permission to mold you, change you, shake you, move you. Little by little you will understand: "He has made everything beautiful in its time" (Eccles. 3:11).

—Kathy Troccoli
Hope for a Woman's Heart

The Messy Mixture of Life

A sun that sets cleanly, without clouds, turns the sky a soft, pretty pink. That kind of sunset is OK but nothing special. In contrast, when there's a messy sky with patches of dark clouds hovering over the horizon to reflect back the full, glorious colors of the sunset, then the sky is streaked with a magnificent spectrum of incredible hues: deep purple, hot pink, velvety gray, flashing crimson, vivid violet, and dozens of other colors. That kind of sunset takes your breath away.

The same is true of life. The messy mixture of sunshine and sorrow, happiness and heartache, triumph and tragedy, rest and toil is not the easiest recipe for a full, vibrant life. But it *is* the recipe. We need to recognize God's presence beside us every step of the way, leading us through the good times, guiding us through the hard times, and carrying us through those times when we couldn't make it on our own.

— **Thelma Wells**
Listen Up, Honey

That Quiet Place

My grandmother was no saint, but she refused to get buried under the load of care she had as a mother, a wife, a church member, a grandmother, and a human being. Every one of those callings has problems attached to it. So how did she do it? She had her own *querencia*. . . .

In Spanish, this word means a favorite and frequent place of rest for wild beasts. . . . I've seen lions . . . in Africa . . . find their *querencia* under trees or near old, rotting logs where there's shade. Life is still hard, and the animals are still ferocious and unpredictable, but they've found just the right spot to spread out and quit battling with the inevitable for a while.

By the same token, we human beings have an undefined place of peace that God offers to us, and we seek it out instinctively. By shifting the weight of tough stuff off our shoulders onto God's, we find that place to relax. It's still a jungle out there, but we unconsciously find that quiet place — our *querencia* — where we stop grinding out life's maddening pace for a few minutes. This spot is inside us, and God makes it available so we can pause and catch our breath. Laugh. Sing. Think. Pray. Everyday rhythms and patterns of life keep going, but we're not going with them.

—Luci Swindoll
Life! Celebrate It

You shall know the truth,
and the truth shall make
you free.

—John 8:32

The Freedom of a Balanced Life

[My husband] grew up in a Norwegian-dominated section of Seattle (Ballard). Mrs. Walvick, who lived next door to his family, was a colorful little lady with predictable patterns and inflexible food habits. Every Saturday morning she went to her special Norwegian bakery, where she bought bread, rolls, and cold cuts for Saturday night sandwiches. Every Saturday morning she'd lean into the butcher's ear for the usual instruction regarding the slicing of her cold cuts. "Not too tick and not too tin," she'd say, stepping back then — confident the butcher knew exactly what she expected from his slicer. . . .

The "not too tick and not too tin" instruction to the butcher could serve me well. Mrs Walvick wanted balance for her cold cuts. That was achieved by not going too far in either direction. This touch of Norwegian wisdom continually inspires me to check my own "tick or tin."

—Marilyn Meberg
Contagious Joy

Skies Filled with Color

$\mathcal{T}$oday, for as far as I can see, there's not a cloud in the sky, not even a wisp. But I know from experience that Texas really knows how to put on a storm. . . .

From sea to shining sea, tempests are to be expected in our weather patterns and in our lives. Try as you might, you can't find a picture-perfect weather spot in the world.

But do we want to? No clouds and no rain equals no green terrain. Why, our gardens would be stubble, our trees stumps, flowers dried-up seeds, and our wells dust. . . .

Clouds are typecast according to how far off the ground they are — high level, midlevel, and low level. Depending on their height, they are composed of water droplets, ice crystals, ice particles, or snow. The moisture content in the clouds, when touched by the light of the evening sun, creates the magnificent array of colors in a sunset.

That's true of our lives as well. Clouds will blow through our neighborhood, whether we live in Texas or Michigan. Some will be fair-weather friends, while others will pummel us with the hail of hardships and swirls of sorrow. While we may have to step through the cleanup, we know the Son will once again fill our skies with color.

—Patsy Clairmont
All Cracked Up

Real ongoing, lifelong education

doesn't answer questions —

it provokes them.

It causes us to see

that the fun and excitement of learning

doesn't lie in having all the answers.

It lies in the tension

and the stretching of our minds

between all the contradictory answers.

It makes us think for ourselves.

It frees us.

—Luci Swindoll

FREE TO BE ME

We are freed, like uncaged birds,
because God loves us
unconditionally.

—Leslie Williams

God Has a Purpose

There are two things I might've changed about my life: I wouldn't have been the youngest in a family of eight (although I can't decide which sibling I could live without!), and I wouldn't have grown up poor.

But we don't always know what we might need in life. There are many positive aspects of my adult life that I can directly attribute to growing up in my family of origin, in our tiny little town.

Because I was little, I learned to speak up. Because I was young, I learned to keep up. And because I was last, I learned to make up the difference. All of that has served me well through the years. When I'm in over my head, I'm comfortable reaching. When I'm overwhelmed, I keep going. When I'm overcommitted, I hang on. Just like my siblings did.

God has His purpose for everything.

—**Mary Graham**
Women of Faith Devotional Bible

Exactly as God Intended

From the time we are rolled into the nursery, foot-printed, blood-typed, and given a birth certificate, we are systematically fed through the tubes of conformity until we lose our distinctive and become another cookie-cutter-two-dimensional-second-cousin-twice-removed version of ourselves. We are told not to laugh too loudly, call attention to ourselves, or make a scene. "Can't you just fit in?"

If you understand who you are and who God made you to be, then it doesn't mess with you when others are who God made them to be. My mom, my daughter, and I share some similarities. We all love ice cream, laugh at chick flicks, love to read books, and believe that any time spent in pajamas is quality time. However, we are totally distinct. My mom L-O-V-E-S to do laundry. I let her! I dress sorta funky; my daughter is more Ann Taylor-ish. My daughter loves hockey; I don't understand it at all. We are all exactly as God intended, and isn't it splendid?

—Anita Renfroe
The Purse-Driven Life

Persons of Great Complexity

A child in Harriet Beecher Stowe's *Uncle Tom's Cabin* was asked, "Do you know who made you?" She speculated. "Nobody, as I knows on," said the child with a short laugh. "I 'spect I jist grow'd."

But the Bible says something very different. One of my favorite verses in Scripture is Jeremiah 1:5: "Before I formed you in the womb I knew you." That is a mind-boggling thought. Before I was ever in the womb of my mother, I was in the mind of my sovereign Creator. What does that mean? God apparently mused, pondered, and thought about my essence and my identity before He called me into being. I am not a composite of haphazardly thrown-together molecules, traits, and characteristics.

God deliberated in the same way, painstakingly and lovingly, over the formation of each of us. We are persons of great complexity and enormous potential, thoughtfully and deliberately formed by the Almighty. We are not creations who "jist grow'd."

God promises that His plan for us is a life of hope, not despair. . . . He does not see us as inadequate or unlovable. He does not reject our true self in favor of whatever façade we've been hiding behind. What a comfort to know that we do not need to be afraid to be who we really are.

— Marilyn Meberg
The Zippered Heart

Each of us has a unique God-given personality to celebrate!

Free to Be Uniquely You

*O*ne of the greatest joys in life is finding out who God made you to be, with all the personality quirks, and loving it. I have always gathered little animals. Growing up as a child in Scotland, we didn't have much money, so my pets were frogs that I caught in the quarry, or worms that I dug up. Often when we arrive at adulthood, we abandon parts of who we are and relegate them to the attic of our mind. I think when we do that, we lose a little piece of ourselves.

Think back to your childhood. What was it that made you unique? How were you different from your siblings? What were the things that you did better than anyone else?

You might be a high-heels girl or a total flip-flop woman. You might love yourself in dresses or only feel at home in jeans. Too often as we grow, we conform too much. Some conformity is necessary to meet job requirement standards or out of respect for others. Where we lose the wonder of who we are, though, is when we conform just to be like others because we are afraid to be different. Different is good!

— Sheila Walsh
I'm Not Wonder Woman

Peace and Joy

Without knowing God and knowing who we
are in Him, we will constantly take our faith on
a roller-coaster ride. It will go up and it will go
down. We'll scream at the treacherous turns
and close our eyes when we start speeding into
a steep downward spiral. Trust doesn't change
God, but it will certainly change the ride. Putting
your complete confidence in Jesus does change
the quality of your life. It affects your peace,
and it affects your joy.

—Kathy Troccoli
Hope for a Woman's Heart

Christ freed me
from all condemnation
when He paid for my failures, mistakes,
and bone-deep naughtiness,
and His forgiveness
offers me the grace
and liberty to forgive others. Whew!

—Patsy Clairmont

Free to Love Me

Let me suggest ten areas I work on when I get bogged down and forget to love myself as God commanded me to. Nobody has a corner on these things, and you already know every one of them by heart. But when you forget, these are reminders:

1. Be content with what you have.
2. Stop comparing.
3. Count your blessings.
4. Quit personalizing every comment.
5. Maintain a servant spirit.
6. Do the unexpected for a loved one.
7. Keep a heart of gratitude.
8. Don't be negative.
9. Respect yourself.
10. Take God at His Word.

—Luci Swindoll
Life! Celebrate It

Start Believing It!

I had to persevere to get through some really trying . . . jobs early in my life. One of the first ones was teaching football players to type — and let me tell you, that was no easy task. Not because football players can't learn typing (or keyboarding, as I suppose we would call it today) but because (1) most of them had hands and fingers so big they needed extra-large keyboards, which don't exist, and (2) most of them didn't want to be there in the first place. They weren't planning to make their living by typing!

Believe me, it took a lot of "I can do all things" prayers to get through that job! . . . But you know what happens when God repeatedly gives you strength to survive overwhelming difficulties? You learn that when the next difficulty comes, He'll give you strength again to persevere. See it proven true a few times that "I can do all things through Christ who strengthens me," and girl, you start believing it!

—Thelma Wells
The Buzz

I CAN DO ALL THINGS
through Christ
who strengthens me.

Believe for the Best

$\mathcal{I}$ live in the first and only house I have ever built and, I'm sure, ever will. It's a once-in-a-lifetime project. When I started, I knew zero about buying a lot and building a house on it. But I punched start, and my desires began to move down the track. I started with what I knew — I called a realtor, hired a builder, began making drawings of what I wanted, talked to the post office about changing my address, wrote letters, sent e-mails, asked questions, and kept going. I started doing what I knew and only that, and when we start there, the unknowns begin to clear up little by little. I acted on an idea and prayer request to God. . . .

We will never get anywhere unless we start. You can quote me on that! If we begin with a feeling or an urge to do something we've never done before, and if we have the confidence and freedom to believe it can be done, then somehow the difficulties attached to it begin to lose their scary power of intimidation. By trusting in God and believing all things are possible with Him, doors to the unknown begin to open; and in time, a sense of certainty sets in. I've had it happen over and over in my life.

—Luci Swindoll
Life! Celebrate It

God's blessings are the
expression of perfect love.

— **Anonymous**

The Ones Who Love

*A*s I've traveled around the country, I've been to a lot of churches that just didn't seem like churches. Once, my family and I went to a service in Chattanooga held in a small church that used to be a bar. . . .

Another time I spoke in a barn that had been turned into a church for a group who called themselves Cowboys for Christ. Every Sunday they would tie up their horses outside, stride (some noticeably bow-legged) into the barn, and sit down hat in hand to hear about God, to worship, and to praise. Then after the service, they would ride. That Sunday they even talked me into jumping on a mare and galloping through a dusty field — in my church dress!

But the real church is the people — the ones who help, . . . the ones who love, the ones who just hang out with you whenever you need someone close.

—Chonda Pierce
I Can See Myself in His Eyeballs

God's purpose is to love us intensely
and lead us intentionally into a broad place
where we can know and enjoy His faithfulness.

—**Mary Graham**

Longing to Be Loved

I know now there is no such thing as perfection on this earth, but as a young girl I saw in others all I wished I could be. I saw how the boys reacted when one of the pretty girls came into a room. I stood awkwardly in gym class as boys chose practice partners for our senior dance, knowing that I would be one of the last chosen.

I turned fifty the summer of 2006. I like my reflection in the mirror now. I am one of those women who looked better at forty than she did at twenty, but every weekend I see young women in my book-signing line, and I recognize myself. I see the unsure half smile, and I hear the silent cry behind their eyes longing to be accepted and loved but braced for rejection. I want to tell each one of them: what changed my life wasn't losing some weight or having my skin clear up; it was touching the hem of Jesus' garment.

—**Sheila Walsh**
I'm Not Wonder Woman

Free to Choose

So many of us have dutifully reproduced our mothers' and fathers' behaviors, duplicating our parents' patterns and manifesting a legacy that we, however unconsciously, feel obligated to fulfill. I want you to know you have a choice: you do not have to haul your parents' legacy into your life like that old dining room set your great aunt left you in her will. If it makes you happy to eat at that table and sit in those chairs, by all means keep them. But if it doesn't, remember: you have options. You can hold on to the table and toss the chairs. Or lose the table and keep the chairs (perhaps reupholster the seats so they're more comfortable). And if you just plain hate the whole thing, get rid of it before you even bring it into the house. Your great aunt's furniture might not suite your dining room, just as your parents' ways of living might not suite your life. You're not insulting your dead aunt by rejecting her old furniture, and you're not betraying your parents by living your life differently than they lived theirs; in fact, what you're doing is being true to yourself.

—Robin McGraw
Inside My Heart

Still Lovable

In loving ourselves unconditionally as God does, we love and accept ourselves based, not on what we *do*, but on who we *are*. There's the tough part. Many of us feel we can perhaps love ourselves if we do something well, if our performance is good. Maybe then we deserve being loved. But how can we love ourselves when we make mistakes and do embarrassing things? That's the whole point; that's the shame-buster element. But if we love ourselves unconditionally, then even when we blow it badly, making huge or small mistakes, we do not waver in our agreement with God that we are still lovable — because He says we are!

—Marilyn Meberg
The Zippered Heart

A single grateful thought

towards heaven

is the most complete prayer.

—G. E. Lessing

Honoring God with My Life

I often talk to women who want to do something adventurous for God but think that unless it's on a grand scale it doesn't count. I say, start where you are with what you have.

When people ask me how I got started as a singer I tell them that I began singing in hospitals and rest homes. With book projects, I began writing stories for my mom when I was a young girl in Scotland. I remember the first story I felt had achieved the status of a classic: "Joey the Budgie Was a Canary."

We place too much emphasis on *ability* when God looks for our *availability* to be used by Him now, with whatever we have.

—Sheila Walsh
The Great Adventure

FREEDOM–
LOVING
FRIENDS

God has choreographed the ballet
and set us free to dance.

—Marva J. Dawn

Delightful Differences

*D*ifferences make for interesting friends. . . .
If your friends were all just like you, life would
be so boring! . . .

One of my good friends is a real
athlete, I mean the kind who takes her
athletic endeavors seriously. When we were
both younger, we played racquetball together.
She had a deadly smash ball that left me
searching and swinging at the air every time
we played. She was a class-A competitor. I have
never been known for my athletic prowess, but
we managed to be friends in spite of this
difference. . . . She didn't get frustrated with me
and I wasn't intimidated by her. We were
friends first and foremost. The differences in our
abilities and our interests were secondary. . . .

Differences make for interesting friends and
allow you to learn from each other.

— Jan Silvious
Big Girls Don't Whine

God's Sweet Counsel

*O*ne of my favorite lighten-up gifts is a shopping spree at a bookstore. Recently, for my birthday, several friends gave me gift cards for a bookstore extravaganza. How fun is that! . . .

I love to read; it broadens my perspective. It takes me off the page I'm living on and opens up new angles of insight. Reading expands my vocabulary, improves my conversational skills, and nudges me away from ingrown opinions.

When we add Scripture to our reading menu, we have the delicious benefit of God's sweet counsel, even when it's startling and goes against our nature. Unsettling as it can be, God's Word prepares me to face scallywags and helps me to survive deeply thrust daggers.

—Patsy Clairmont
All Cracked Up

Jesus spoke of freedom,
but He spoke of a
different kind
of freedom:
the type of freedom that
comes not through power
but through submission.
Not through control
but through surrender.
Not through possessions
but through open hands.

—Max Lucado

Gifts to Give for Free

 The gift of listening: No interrupting, no daydreaming, no planning a response . . . just listening.

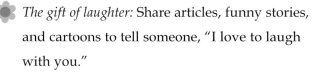 *The gift of laughter:* Share articles, funny stories, and cartoons to tell someone, "I love to laugh with you."

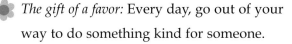 *The gift of a compliment:* A simple and sincere word of praise can make someone's day.

 The gift of a favor: Every day, go out of your way to do something kind for someone.

 The gift of a cheerful disposition: You can never give away too many smiles and kind words.

The gift of prayer: Let friends and loved ones know you pray for them — and then do it.

— Anonymous

God made you to be amazing!

A Listening Heart

We do two types of listening. One is listening for mere facts. . . .This is the kind of listening we do in classes, in business, or in committee meetings. We listen for information. The other kind of listening we could call empathetic listening. With this kind of listening we not only hear the facts — the words — but we also hear the heart and the soul behind the words.

An empathetic listener is a great antidote for someone suffering from a broken spirit and dry bones. I recall times when I have been so ministered to by a friend with the gift of empathetic listening that my broken spirit was mended merely by being heard. I feel loved and affirmed when someone hears my soul. It renews my confidence and restores my peace. It also increases my sense of lightheartedness and my inclination to laugh.

—Marilyn Meberg
Choosing the Amusing

A friend is a gift
you give yourself.

—R. L. Stevenson

I Choose Love

*B*ecause of Calvary, I'm free to choose. And so I choose.

I choose love . . .

No occasion justifies hatred; no injustice warrants bitterness. I choose love. Today I will love God and what God loves.

I choose joy . . .

I will invite my God to be the God of circumstance. I will refuse the temptation to be cynical. . . . I will refuse to see any problem as anything less than an opportunity to see God.

I choose peace . . .

I will live forgiven. I will forgive so that I may live. . . .

I choose gentleness . . .

Nothing is won by force. I choose to be gentle. If I raise my voice may it be only in praise. . . .

I choose self-control . . .

I will be impassioned only by my faith. I will be influenced only by God. I will be taught only by Christ. I choose self-control.

Love, joy, peace, patience, kindness, goodness, faithfulness, gentleness, and self-control. To these I commit my day. If I succeed, I will give thanks. If I fail, I will seek God's grace. And then, when this day is done, I will place my head on my pillow and rest.

—Max Lucado
When God Whispers Your Name

Girlfriends know they can't fix every hurt

or soothe every pain.

They know that prayer is the best thing

they can do for a friend;

holding her hand is second.

—Jan Silvious

Refining Touches

Recently, a major chocolate company teamed up with a high-fashion shoe designer. The companies waged a national contest in which the top prize included luscious chocolates and thousands of dollars in shoes. The gal who won just happened to be from a family with two other sisters and a mom, and — get this! — they all wore the same size shoe. What fun! . . .

The Bible speaks of footwear, but even more of our walk. Especially our walk. . . . Consider Ruth, who, during her time of stepping through the valley of the shadow of death when her husband died, chose to follow her mother-in-law to a new land — a land where Ruth would know no one, look different, and spend her days serving her broken and bitter mother-in-law. While that may sound like Ruth made a hasty choice, God intervened on her behalf and made provisions for her that would lead her into a loving marriage and even restore her mother-in-law's joy. Ruth's story is a good reminder. . . . While loss doesn't seem like a friend, it often brings refining touches to our character.

— **Patsy Clairmont**
All Cracked Up

Free to Tell the Truth

When a dear friend who obviously loves her new dress asks if you think it makes her look fat, and the ruffles at the hip line do indeed accentuate a part of the anatomy best left unnoticed, do you say, "No, the dress is flattering," or do you say, "Honey, as quickly as you possibly can you need to return that dress — and stop by Weight Watchers on your way home"?

Let's consider this friend. . . . Why would I lie and compliment her on the dress when in reality I'm horrified? Because I fear her displeasure and her disappointment, which I fear may be acted out on me in the form of a pouting morbid silence. My opinion would be rejected and her disappointment would also lead to a rejection of me. That rejection might not last forever, but who wants to ruin a perfectly good lunch while waiting for her to snap out of it? Peace at any price — pass the pizza! . . .

But when I lie, I pay a price. I not only pay the price of a loss of trust from those who know the lie is a lie, but I also lose personal dignity. . . . The deepest problem with lying is that it is in direct opposition to the divine imprint within me. When I don't tell the truth, I lose a measure of personal dignity, which in turn robs me of self-esteem. . . . The act of lying is in essence a form of treachery against the human spirit.

—Marilyn Meberg
The Zippered Heart

Freedom and Friendship

Friendship is a wonderful thing. I cannot imagine a day going by without talking with my friends. . . . Ralph Waldo Emerson asserted that there are two cornerstones to friendship. One is truth, the other tenderness. I agree. To love someone, we must know they are truthful with us. Love is built on respect and respect on trust. Truth and tenderness must go hand in hand because if they try to stand alone, one will be too hard and the other too soft.

I would add a third element that is essential to friendship — freedom. We can love others tenderly, be completely truthful with them, but unwittingly want them as our own. We find ourselves hurt if they do things with other people and we're not included. If we don't encourage them to be free (even of us), there is no real friendship. When we hold on to anything too tightly, it dies.

—Luci Swindoll
I Married Adventure

We need to build bridges

between our hearts

and those of people

we see who need a friend—

and allow Jesus

to cross that bridge of friendship

and walk into their lives.

—Max Lucado

THANKFULLY FREE!

One way to develop the joyful habit
is to nurture an attitude
of thankfulness.

— Barbara Johnson

With Song and Dancing

*O*ne way or another, we all need some applause and praise in our lives. And guess what: so does God. Again and again, the Bible tells us to praise our Creator. Read the Psalms, and you'll see that we're to praise God with song, with dancing, with tambourines and harps, with trumpet blasts and loud cymbals — and I'm sure He wouldn't mind a little applause now and then either. . . .

After all, God made us in His image, and since we like to hear applause, that must mean He does too! When's the last time you prayed simply to praise God?

— Barbara Johnson
Contagious Joy

PRAISE GOD

Hearty Laughter

*A*ccording to some joyologists (uh-huh, *joyologists* — those given to the promotion of joy), you can lose weight if you guffaw daily. So does this mean we can titter till our tummies tuck? Or better yet, chortle till the cellulite runs smooth? I'm afraid I'd have to be permanently hysterical to accomplish that task. . . .

Have you ever wondered why God designed us with the ability to laugh and cry? I guess He knew we would need to do both as a way to pour off emotional excess; otherwise, we might blow a gasket. And gasket blowing is so untidy.

I've heard it said that hearty laughter sends fresh shipments of oxygen to the brain, which causes it to loosen up. Hmm, if it can loosen up my brain, then maybe, just maybe, the joyologists are right, and it could loosen up my jeans. That would be great. Then I wouldn't have to unsnap them to eat, sit, travel, and breathe.

— Patsy Clairmont
All Cracked Up

I view laughter as an intensifier of joy.
When we experience laughter as well as joy, we
double our pleasure!

—Marilyn Meberg

LOVE

Loved by God

God wants our hearts. He doesn't want our activity alone, our busyness, our long list of things we have done for Him; He wants *us*. I am still amazed by this, but I hold it to be the dearest truth of my life that the God of the universe wants my heart. No matter what our culture, or at times the Church, tells us about what really matters, this truth remains: God loves us, and it is His driving passion to be loved by us. You were made for nothing less.

—Sheila Walsh
I'm Not Wonder Woman

The Enormous Love of God

Every Friday that I'm not on the road, [my writing assistant], Karen, and I go to Starbucks and work on my latest writing project. As you might expect, we begin by ordering a *grande* skinny mocha with whipped cream for me, and a *grande* hot chocolate for her. Then we settle in at a tiny table for a three-hour chat on the finer and deeper things of life. We grapple with all we don't understand, we consider truths, we wonder about apparent inconsistencies, and eventually we end up pondering the enormous love of God. We both marvel at the greatness and goodness of God. When we really try to fathom our amazing Savior, it's incomprehensible — all we can do is praise.

That's what heaven will be — a place of purpose. A place to eternally ponder and praise the goodness and greatness of our God. . . . I believe that we will marvel at our Savior, ponder His great love for us, and praise. Praise quietly, praise loudly. Heaven will be the place in which we worship forever.

— Jennifer Rothschild
Lessons I Learned in the Light

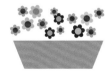

Do Something Fun!

*H*ow do you react to life's unpleasant circumstances? Do you look for ways to find happiness and joy or do you just give in . . . give up, and join the ranks of the "if-anything-bad-can-happen-it-will-happen-to-me" people? Granted, every dilemma doesn't have a humorous side, but I believe more do than we realize.

Here are a few principles that have helped me thrive through disappointments, turning around a difficult circumstance. Remember these when the chips are down:

 Realize most problems are inconveniences, not catastrophes.

 Don't take yourself too seriously, and stop being so literal.

 Count your blessings instead of your blunders.

Take everything as a compliment.

 Enjoy your freedom because Christ has set you free.

Look for the funny side of everything even if it's teensy-weensy.

Don't sweat the small stuff.

Do something fun just for yourself that makes you laugh.

—Luci Swindoll
Life! Celebrate It

Rejoice in the Lord always;
again I will say, rejoice.

Philippians 4:4

Freedom from Bad Attitudes

Attitude is everything and whatever is going on in life the way we respond is crucial. Paul is not being redundant when he says, "Rejoice, and again I say *rejoice*." He effectively creates a picture for us. Imagine the sight of a little lamb coming out of the barn and jumping up once, then jumping up again. He leaps across the fields and hills, jumping as if for the sheer fun of it. So we are to rejoice and keep on rejoicing, *not* because things are wonderful, but because of the joy that comes from knowing the Lord is in the middle of things that are going on.

No matter how much you might want to be like Scarlet O'Hara and deal with life's realities *tomorrow*, that is no way to live. No matter your circumstances, rejoice and rejoice again, because God is the author and finisher of life. He is in the middle of everything you face, no matter what.

—Jan Silvious
Big Girls Don't Whine

Blessed
are the
joymakers.

—N. P. Willis

God's Opportunity

Okay, so maybe it's easier to spot God, to recognize His presence, when something good happens, like at a baby christening or a revival or a wedding. But can I see God in the hard times? The ugly times? Like when I get a speeding ticket, or when my daughter wrecks her grandfather's truck? . . . Where is God in all that?

No long ago I read a devotional by Charles Henry Parkhurst, a nineteenth-century minister who wrote about young David slaying a lion long before he ever fought Goliath. The lion, Parkhurst said, was "God's opportunity in disguise." Had David not succeeded there, he might never have faced Goliath (probably because he would have been that lion's lunch). Then I read, "May the Lord open our eyes to see Him, even in temptations, trials, dangers, and misfortunes."

So God makes Himself known when we are in an angry lion's presence. But — we have to open our eyes.

—Chonda Pierce
I Can See Myself in His Eyeballs

Start with a Grateful Heart

When I'm tempted to gripe, I have to start talking to myself. And when I come to my senses, this is what I say: "Luci, if you can't be content in this moment of inconvenience, be content that it's not worse. Shut up and count your blessings."

But there are times I can't pull myself out of that morass until I *start with a grateful heart*. Our constant attitude should be gratitude. But it seems to be the rarest of virtues. God has given us thousands of reasons to celebrate life every day, even in the worst of times, if we just open our eyes, live in the moment, take in the beauty, and see the possibilities.

—**Luci Swindoll**
Life! Celebrate It

COUNT YOUR BLESSINGS

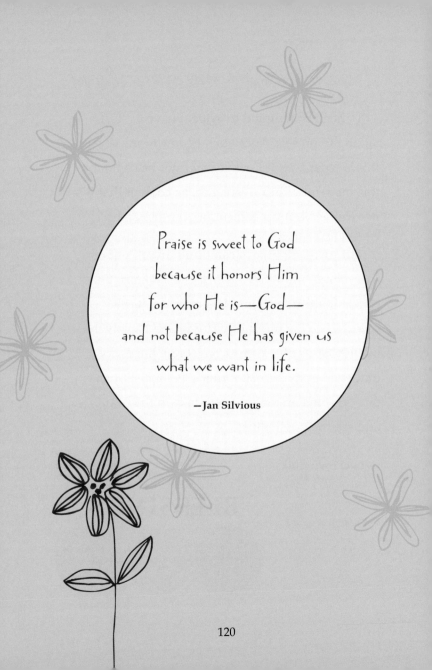

Praise is sweet to God
because it honors Him
for who He is—God—
and not because He has given us
what we want in life.

—Jan Silvious

Beautiful and Amazing

When you look in a mirror, what do you see? What are the things that your eyes gravitate toward? How critical are you when you look at yourself? What are the tapes that play over and over in your head?

God our Father is thinking about us every day. When God thinks about us, His thoughts are 100 percent accurate. He doesn't think we are smarter than we are or less able than we are. He doesn't think we are as godly as the image we try to present at times when we are feeling spiritual or dismiss us as hopeless wretches when that is how we feel. God knows all that is true and loves us totally. So we don't struggle with what God thinks; we struggle with what *we* think.

God's Word never changes. He always sees us as beautiful and amazing; it is we who change as the world around us changes. Our challenge is to keep the image of the woman God sees more prominent than the image of the woman we see with our human eyes.

—Sheila Walsh
I'm Not Wonder Woman

Free to Listen and Learn

When I read the story of Solomon [in the book of 2 Chronicles], I'm inspired to listen and learn. I'm also intrigued by another character who entered the picture. In studying these Scripture passages, I've decided that if Solomon was the wisest man, the queen of Sheba had to be the wisest woman. Why? Because when she heard about King Solomon's wisdom, she loaded up a huge caravan and made her way to Jerusalem to listen and learn from him.

She was amazed by what he told her. She said, "I did not believe what they said until I came and saw with my own eyes. Indeed, not even half the greatness of your wisdom was told me; you have far exceeded the report I heard" (2 Chronicles 9:6 NIV).

Let's be like the queen of Sheba and seek out wisdom, even if it seems inconvenient or even if we think we're too busy or too old or already smart enough. Let's keep our spirits tuned to the frequency of the still, small voice of God giving us guidance and knowledge. Let's listen and learn.

—Thelma Wells
Listen Up, Honey

Other Books by Women of Faith

Irrepressible Hope
Faith for a Lifetime
Contagious Joy
Amazing Freedom

By Patsy Clairmont
I Grew Up Little
All Cracked Up
Dancing Bones

By Marilyn Meberg
God at Your Wits' End
Since You Asked
Free Inside and Out

By Luci Swindoll
Notes to a Working Woman
Life! Celebrate It
Free Inside and Out

By Sheila Walsh
Extraordinary Faith
I'm Not Wonder Woman
God Has a Dream for Your Life

By Thelma Wells
The Buzz
Listen Up, Honey
What These Girls Knew

Acknowledgments

Grateful acknowledgment is made to the following publishers for permission to reprint this copyrighted material.

Patsy Clairmont ©, *All Cracked Up* (Nashville: W. Publishing Group, 2006)

Patsy Clairmont et al. ©, *The Great Adventure* (Nashville: W. Publishing Group, 2002)

Patsy Clairmont et al. ©, *Contagious Joy* (Nashville: W. Publishing Group, 2006)

Barbara Johnson ©, *Daily Splashes of Joy* (Nashville: W. Publishing Group, 2000).

Barbara Johnson ©, *Leaking Laffs Between Pampers and Depends* (Nashville: W. Publishing Group, 2000).

Max Lucado ©, *When God Whispers Your Name* (Nashville: W. Publishing Group, 1994)

Max Lucado ©, *Come Thirsty* (Nashville: W. Publishing Group, 2004)

Max Lucado ©, *Cure for the Common Life* (Nashville: W. Publishing Group, 2005)

Marilyn Meberg ©, *The Zippered Heart* (Nashville: W. Publishing Group, 2001)

Chonda Pierce ©, *Roadkill on the Highway to Heaven* (Grand Rapids: Zondervan, 2006)

Anita Renfroe ©, *The Purse-Driven Life* (Colorado Springs: NavPress, 2005)

Jennifer Rothschild ©, *Lessons I Learned in the Light* (Colorado Springs: Multnomah Publishers, Inc., 2006)

Jan Silvious ©, *Big Girls Don't Whine* (Nashville: W. Publishing Group, 2003)

Luci Swindoll ©, *I Married Adventure* (Nashville: W. Publishing Group, 2002)

Luci Swindoll ©, *Life! Celebrate It* (Nashville: W. Publishing Group, 2006)

Kathy Troccoli ©, *Hope for a Woman's Heart* (Nashville: J Countryman, 2002).

Sheila Walsh ©, *The Heartache No One Sees* (Nashville: Thomas Nelson, Inc., 2004)

Sheila Walsh ©, *Outrageous Love* (Nashville: J Countryman, 2004)

Sheila Walsh ©, *I'm Not Wonder Woman* (Nashville: Thomas Nelson, Inc., 2006)

Thelma Wells ©, *The Buzz* (Nashville: W Publishing Group, 2000)

Thelma Wells ©, *Listen Up, Honey* (Nashville: W Publishing Group, 2004)

Women of Faith ©, *Women of Faith Devotional Bible* (Nashville: Thomas Nelson Bibles, 2003)

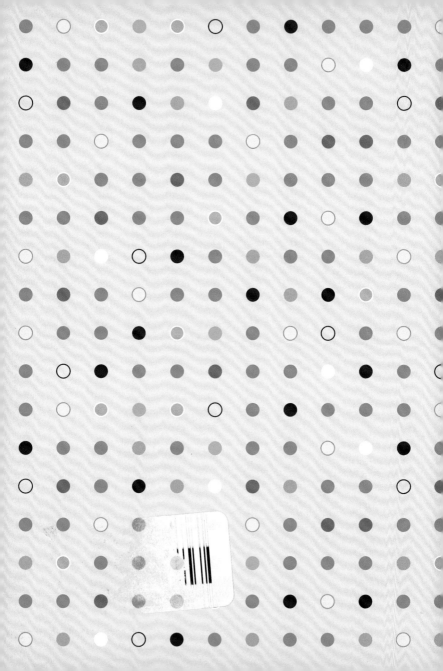